TWEEN TIME

A TWEEN'S GUIDE TO ACADEMIC SUCCESS

ERAINNA WINNETT, Ed.S.

Tween Time: A Tween's Guide to ACADEMIC SUCCESS
Text © 2014 Erainna Winnett
Cover Design Chamillah Designs
Interior Design Streetlight Graphics

Library of Congress: Cataloging-in-Publication Data
Winnett, Erainna
Tween Time: A Tween's Guide to ACADEMIC SUCCESS
Summary: Discusses issues facing children aged 9-12 as they
struggle with academics preparation and success.
Test Preparation—Juvenile self-help. 2. Homework Help—Juvenile self-help.
3. Study Skills. Juvenile self-help 4. Organization. Juvenile-self-help

ISBN-13: 978-0692213247
ISBN-10: 0692213244

CounselingwithHEART.com

Printed in the United States of America
10 9 8 7 6 5 4 3 2 1

DEDICATION

To Ashley and Amber,

my two girls

To accomplish great things, we must not only act, but also dream, not only plan, but also believe.

– Anatole France

THIS BOOK BELONGS TO:

A tween whose first step toward academic success begins TODAY!

TWEEN TIME ACADEMIC SUCCESS

A TWEEN'S GUIDE TO ACADEMIC SUCCESS

WHY SHOULD YOU READ THIS BOOK?
BECAUSE IT WILL HELP YOU WITH THE FOLLOWING:

- **Homework Help!** Discover how to set up a place and an attitude so you can complete your homework in a snap.

- **Finding Time for Fun Time!** Learn how to better manage the balance between fun time and academic time.

- **Optimal Organization!** Create fun ways to keep your life organized, including schoolwork and your social life.

- **Test-Prep Tips!** Explore ways to prep for tests to get the best grades you can.

- **Study Skills!** Find out which ways are the *most effective* to improve your study habits.

If you take the time to read this book and follow the tips and strategies it contains, there's no telling just how great a student you'll become. The sky's the limit on this one, so dream big because *you can do it*!

GETTING THE MOST FROM THIS BOOK

3 MUST-DO TIPS FOR READING THIS BOOK:

✓ **Tip #1:** Here's a phrase for you to remember: *A chapter a day keeps success on the way!* Read just one chapter each day at whatever time of day is best for *you* to read. A chapter a day gives you some time to think about what you've read rather than just rushing through it all and then not remembering the important stuff! It will help the content stick where you need it most, which is *in* your head (as opposed to *on* your head, which would look silly).

✓ **Tip #2:** Here's another phrase to remember: *Slow it down!* If you read a whole chapter in any *less* than 30 minutes, you're reading way too fast. Slow down! You want this material to really sink in, so take your time with it. You'll also have a better time answering some of the questions that will really get you thinking about the best ways to keep track of everything you need and want to do.

✓ **Tip #3:** Finally, you want to be sure to put this book in a special place after you're done reading it. Then mark a calendar for the week before school will start *next year*. Why am I asking you to do this? Because you're going to read the book AGAIN before school starts next year. You may think I've gone off the deep end, but hear me out. This book is going to put you on the pathway to success in both your school life and your home life, which means you'll want to be reminded of it all just before starting school again next year. Trust me, you'll be really glad you took this advice!

TABLE OF CONTENTS

INTRODUCTION

HAVE YOU EVER WISHED YOU could get better grades or just be better at schoolwork? You're not alone! I've met a LOT of kids your age, and I can tell you from experience that most kids want to be more successful at school. The problem is that a whole lot of things just seem to get in the way. Between regular homework, special projects and assignments, sports, clubs, playing an instrument, after-school activities, chores around the house, and spending time with friends, it feels as though there's no way to fit it all in. Schoolwork and grades are often among the first things to suffer when you're feeling overwhelmed with trying to keep it all under control.

I'm here to tell you that *there is a better way*—a much *less stressful* way to go about not only getting everything done that you *have* to do, but also finding time to do the things you really *want* to do. This book will show you how.

You're probably thinking to yourself, "Yeah, right, lady. That sounds too good to be true!" And you're right. It *is* too good to be true if what you're hoping for is some kind of magic bullet or fairy godmother (or a fairy

godmother with a magic bullet—now, there's an interesting thought) that fixes everything without any effort on your part. If *that's* what you were hoping for, I'm sorry to say that's not what this book is about. Getting everything done *and* having time for fun simply has to involve some real work on your part. The good news, however, is that the benefits of following the tips and strategies I'm going to share far outweigh the effort you have to put into making it happen. Trust me on this one, you'll be a MUCH happier and more successful kid if you take the time to read and do what's in this book. And all the grown-ups around you will be super impressed with what you're doing!

That's why I wrote this book for you. I have seen firsthand how hard life can be for tweens. I've worked with kids your age for the past twenty years as not only a teacher, but also as an elementary school counselor. I've even raised two of my own kids. I've seen lots of tweens really struggle with how to balance school, home, and friends. And I've learned a few things along the way that I think will help you be much more successful in everything you do!

CHAPTER 1: OPTIMAL ORGANIZATION

YOU'VE SEEN WHAT HAPPENS WHEN people don't keep things organized, right? You know those kids—the ones who open their lockers and all this stuff comes tumbling out. Stuffing it all back in usually makes them late for whatever it is they're supposed to be going to. Then there are the kids who keep really messy desks. They can never find what they need next, which wastes everyone's time. And, of course, there are kids who have really unorganized, messy binders, which means they have trouble finding the homework that's due, if they even remembered to put it in their binder in the first place.

Have you ever seen kids who are that unorganized? If there were an award for being messy, they would definitely win it. It's both embarrassing and painful to be in that situation. If you *are* one of those kids, don't worry! Help is on the way. In fact, you're holding it in your hands right now. Even if you're not an award-winning messy kid, most tweens I know could definitely use some improvement in these areas. And this book is going to help you do just that.

It's very important to learn how to organize yourself in the most effective way. The word OPTIMAL means MOST. In other words, we're not trying to just be a *little* more organized—we're going for being the *most* organized student and person you can be. Why? You're just now entering a new chapter of school and your life, which is being a TWEEN. Getting organized needs to become a very important part of your day-to-day routine. If you have trouble keeping things in the right place or you find it difficult to keep yourself organized and tidy, you probably know that it can be very *stressful* when your parents or teachers ask you to clean up. Sometimes it's just not that simple. That's why I'm going to share some tips and tricks for how *you* can get organized and stay that way!

FROM CHORES ≠ FUN TO CHORES = FUN

A LOT OF KIDS YOUR age think chores are a big waste of time. But did you know that even adults don't like to do chores? It's not just kids who feel that way! *Everybody* wants to have time to relax when they get home after a long day. If you're one of those kids who finds chores super frustrating, you know how exhausting it is to be told over and over that this or that needs to be done in a certain way. What's cool, though, is that you don't have to take that so personally. You can choose to separate yourself from the chore you have to do. Yes, you have to get it done in a certain way, but *you* are in charge of how you get to the finish line of properly completing it. You can transform your chores by asking these questions:

- *Is there any way to make this chore fun or exciting?*

- *What can be done to make it go by faster?*

- *How will you entertain yourself while you're completing this chore? Can you listen to music or sing a little tune to yourself?*

- *When does the chore have to be completed?*

- *What do you get to do after the chore is done? Should you be focusing on that while you work in order to take your mind off things?*

This is a great list of questions to ask yourself when you're trying to figure out how to switch up the tired routine of chores. Do you remember the movie *Mary Poppins*? That catchy song with the lyrics that say *a spoonful of sugar helps the medicine go down* was really onto something. Mary Poppins says that in everything that must be done, there is an element of fun. And she's right. If you can just find what's fun in the chore you have to do, it'll go by *much* faster!

The number one reason chores are so frustrating, especially for kids your age, is that it almost feels like punishment. Many chores are not very fun and are usually things kids like you don't want to be doing on a daily basis. You have to try and find creative and different ways to make them fun. After all, there are no magic spells for making chores go away. You can't say "Abracadabra, chores away!" and have your chores disappear just because you want them to, although it's a nice little fantasy, isn't it?

THE SAME FORMULA FOR HOMEWORK

HOMEWORK ORGANIZATION IS AN IMPORTANT part of every student's life. If you're not able to organize your stuff when you get home for the day, how are you going to be able to figure out what to do first?

If you can learn to organize your schoolwork by *prioritizing* what is most important or what will take the longest, you can complete any assignment with ease. What follows is a list of questions and responses that will help you figure out if you have a good system in place for organizing your homework, both at home and at school. This will become increasingly important as you move up through the grades after elementary school. Now is the time to get it right!

✓ *Do you have a binder or tags for each of your subjects? Do they go in any particular order?*

✓ *What type of backpack do you have? Can it fit all your supplies for the day easily, or does it become too full after a while?*

✓ *Can you list all the assignments you have for the next week off the top of your head?*

✓ *If you answered NO to the previous question, are you keeping any sort of planner or calendar where you write down the dates of tests and assignments?*

✓ *Do you think it would help your study skills if you had a planner or calendar? Why or why not?*

DIY TOOLS FOR OPTIMAL ORGANIZATION

DIY IS AN ACRONYM THAT stands for Do-It-Yourself. It's another way of saying *homemade*. Creating your own tools for optimal organization is a fun way to get everyone involved with building up your organizing skills. Below are two great ways to make some unique tools for organizing your home life. By sharing this information with your classmates, friends, and parents, you can get them thinking along the same lines. Once you see the fun in being organized, you'll wonder why you waited so long to do it!

DIY HOME CALENDAR

USING A LARGE DRY-ERASE BOARD or piece of large poster board (in any color you like), you can make your own personal calendar to hang in your room. By creating one for each month, you'll be able to look at all the different due dates, tests, and other important school activities you have coming up—and hanging it up in your room means there's no possible way you could *not* see it, right? Making a calendar is also a great opportunity to get a little creativity on with your arts and crafts skills, which makes this activity even more fun. Here's what you'll need:

✓ Dry-erase board or poster board

✓ Dry-erase markers

✓ Permanent marker

✓ Plain or funky-shaped scissors

✓ Glue

✓ Glitter, feathers, or other fun stuff

✓ Double-sided tape

✓ Long ruler or yardstick for drawing straight lines

Ask your parents to borrow a calendar so you have a guide to work from. You're basically going to create the same thing, drawing a grid to label the days of the week and all the days for that month. The only difference is that it's going to be *bigger* so you have room to write in each day's square what you need to remember. If you chose to use the dry-erase board, you'll use the permanent marker to draw your grid. This way you can erase each month's assignments without erasing the grid lines. Then you can have as much fun as you want decorating your calendar, coloring patterns on it, cutting stuff out of magazines to glue onto it, and adding stickers or glitter. The sky's the limit, so have fun! Just remember that each

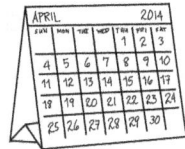

square needs to have enough room for writing several things. If you fill it up with too many cool decorations, you might wind up with a calendar that doesn't have enough room on it to be useful for what you need it to do in the first place!

DIY DESK ORGANIZER

WHEN YOU GET HOME FROM school after a long day you're probably going to have to finish your homework before any actual fun can happen. Maybe you get to play first, but eventually the time for homework will come around, which can leave you feeling frustrated. Usually, parents help choose a spot that is your homework space. If you don't have a desk or area you can customize for homework, you can skip this one. However, if you do have a desk and you need ways to keep your stuff organized while you're studying, there are many different things you can do. The most important of all is to know that it's very easy to create these types of tools. All it takes is a little bit of creativity and inspiration to make it happen. Here are some of the basic things you can use:

✓ Paper towel tubes cut in half for pencil storage

✓ Tissue boxes serve as nice storage bins for all kinds of supplies

✓ Any small boxes you can find around the house

✓ A shoebox can be cut in half for holding things

✓ Small jars and cups

No matter what types of tools you use when you're designing your desk environment, the most important thing to remember is to make an environment you actually want to work in. If you're going to be constantly distracted by your siblings or if your desk is in an area that gets a lot of foot traffic from your family, ask your parents to move it for you. If that's not possible, it may be time to think about other places to do your homework. A big part of homework is organization, and it can be hard to focus and concentrate on being organized when you're distracted by everything going on around you. Some great examples of other places you can go to do homework are the public library, the school library, a relative's house with a quieter atmosphere, or a friend's house where you can work on tasks together. No matter where you decide to go, what's important is that you find different ways to get the work done.

Today many assignments are web-based. If your homework involves using the computer make sure you spend your time actually doing homework. I know it's extremely challenging to sit in front of a computer or tablet and NOT want to get social or play games. Being social and playing games is a whole lot of fun, but NOT during homework time. Make sure to dedicate homework time to homework!

BACKPACK + BINDER = AWESOME!

JUST AS BEING ORGANIZED WITH your homework is important, backpack and binder organization is an essential concept that everyone can learn. Sometimes people become careless with their backpacks and binders, allowing them to become messy. In the case of a backpack, it can be disastrous when it's loaded with way too much junk or with food that leaks and spills. Once you have a mess in your backpack, it can become impossible to clean out. By learning how to keep it organized and staying on top of your things and what you need to do, you'll have a lot less stress in your life! There are ways to make organizing your backpack and binder fun and exciting, but first you have to ask yourself a few important questions.

BACKPACK BASICS

IN THIS SECTION, WE'LL GO over how to keep your backpack neat and clean and what you could be doing differently. Optimal organization results when we learn from our own mistakes. Don't get upset if you don't like your answer to a particular question. Everybody has issues at one time or another, especially around being organized. It's about finding a routine or pattern of keeping things tidy that works for *you*. The following questions will also help you decide if you're using the right size of backpack and, if you're not, how to approach the topic with your parents. Circle your answers.

Do you feel as though your bag is too heavy or is constantly overloaded?

Yes   No   Sometimes

How many binders and notebooks do you keep in your backpack?

1–2   2–3   3–4   4–5

More than five   None at all

How often do you clean out your backpack?

Every day   Every couple of days   Weekly

Monthly   Never

WHAT THE ANSWERS MEAN

YOU'RE GOING TO WONDER HOW I could tell so much about you just by asking you a few simple, short questions.

Do you feel as though your bag is too heavy or is constantly overloaded?

If you answered yes to this question, you might have more to worry about than just a lot of homework. If your bag has become heavy to the point of causing you physical pain, it's time to speak with a parent or other adult about finding a new one. This situation can cause serious back problems, so make sure to fix the situation as soon as possible. If you're not able to get a new backpack right away, you might want to try putting less into the main pockets and keeping more things at home. If the weight of your binder has become the main issue, try separating your work into separate folders that will be lighter and easier to carry.

Things like lunch bags and equipment for playing outdoors can be carried by hand instead of stuffed into a backpack. All in all, your backpack should be a place for school materials only, not a dumping ground for anything and everything. Keep this in mind when you start to feel an ache in your back and consider cleaning it out. Better to be safe than sorry when it comes to your back!

How many binders and notebooks do you keep in your backpack?

If you answered anywhere between 1 and 4, that's fantastic. The more small binders or folders you're able to keep your materials in, the easier it becomes to stay organized and ready for any challenge that comes your way. Because each course is different from the others, the ability to separate your work is a very important lesson that all young people should learn. It will become a great tool when you're trying to study for tests or keep things in different places for the sake of assignments.

If you have more than 4 notebooks in your backpack, that's okay, but you may want to take some time to consolidate some of the work. It can be hard on your back and the rest of your body to carry all those notebooks around, even if you're being super organized about your schoolwork. If you answered none at all and you're simply throwing papers into your backpack at the end of each day, it's time to make a change. If you're going to be organized in the future, you have to start forming habits *now* that will stick with you.

How often do you clean out your backpack?

Cleaning out your backpack is a very important part of staying fresh and organized. It will keep you prepared for the day at hand and can be very valuable when you have to squeeze in last-minute items. By keeping a clean and tidy backpack, not only will you impress your parents, but you'll also feel a difference in what you carry around to and from school. For this question, if you answered anywhere from every day to weekly, you've already learned how to keep your backpack clean. If you answered anything longer than weekly, it's time to learn the ropes of keeping your backpack in shape.

BUT CLEANING MY BACKPACK IS A CHORE!

HAVING A CLEAN BACKPACK HELPS you have a clear mind. You just never know what the day will bring or what surprises are in store, so having a clean backpack means you're prepared for anything. It may sound silly, but it's true! This is true for all our different spaces—an uncluttered space is a reflection of a clear mind.

Besides, if you're keeping too much stuff in your backpack because you never clean it out, it's literally weighing you down! This is when you might end up with a sore back.
to clean it out. You'll feel bet
lighter on you—you'll be able to
to the ice cream truck after
school with a lighter backpack.
What? Your school doesn't

have an ice cream truck waiting outside for you every day? Hmmmm ... I'll have to look into that for you!

A clean backpack and binder will also help you stay organized in many different ways. When something is clean and organized, you'll be more tempted to keep it that way, and eventually it will become a habit that you don't even think about. By using your homemade calendar, mark the days when you can clean out your backpack and binder. Sometimes you don't even need to put it on the schedule if you think you'll remember. Simply try and keep the mess out of your backpack and binder or fix it when you first notice it. By putting it off and trying to come back and fix the problem later, it may get even worse.

BINDER BASICS

A BINDER IS AN ESSENTIAL part of your learning tool kit. It can help you keep your schoolwork separate and will give you all the resources you need in order to achieve your maximum potential. By having a tidy binder, you can study efficiently and keep your assignments together in one spot. Some kids choose to have multiple binders for all their schoolwork and carry those around in their backpacks. At the beginning of the day, you can bring in multiple binders for each subject and leave them all in your desk, locker, or cubby space. If, at the end of the day, you only have homework in two out of five classes, only bring those two binders home with you. When it comes to organizing your school materials, the options are endless. Try the following tips when you're building your new binder or set of binders.

✓ Use dividers for your work. If you buy multicolored dividers, you'll be able to make each subject a color, like green for math, red for social studies, and so on.

✓ Keep a schedule in each binder so you know what you're supposed to be doing and when you're supposed to be doing it for that subject.

✓ Clean out any stray papers daily or weekly.

✓ Three-hole-punch blank pieces of paper or slide them into a side pocket so they aren't loose.

✓ Buy a binder with lots of different pockets and folds so you have plenty of storage space.

✓ Look around your local office supply store to find the binder that works best for you.

Following these tips can lead you to find out what type of binder will work best for you and help you keep everything optimally organized for success in school. That, in turn, will spill over into the rest of your life, where you can also enjoy being more organized.

OPTIMAL ORGANIZATION FOR YOUR LOCKER

LOCKERS CAN BE AN EXCITING part of a student's school experience when it's the first time you get to use one. Up until the point when you get a locker, you probably just had a rack or some kind of storage space where you could hang up your coat and backpack every day. Compared to that, a locker is like a whole new world! It can be where lots of different things happen throughout your day. This is why you want to always keep it organized and have everything you'll need during the day at the ready. Having a messy locker can throw your whole day off track, not to mention really embarrass you, depending on what kind of mess you have going in there. Anything smelly or stinky is what you really want to avoid, right? Few things are more embarrassing than having someone announce loudly in the hallway, "Is that smell coming from *your* locker? That's so gross!" You don't want to be known as the kid with a stinky locker, do you?

I remember when I was in sixth grade one of my classmates was the messy kind of kid, and my locker was right next to his. Just before Christmas break, he left one of his uneaten sack lunches in his locker. The day we came back to school, I walked up to my locker and thought I was going to puke from the smell. For one very panicky moment, I thought the smell might be coming from *my* locker. Thank goodness it wasn't, but boy, was that kid embarrassed about having a stinky locker!

Keeping your locker organized can help you in many different ways. For one, if you buy a bunch of supplies from your local office store when it comes time to go back to school, you can keep your locker organized and customize it at the same time. Things like colorful magnets, mirrors, book shelves, supply organizers, and much more can help keep all your things together inside your locker. If you're sharing your locker with someone else in your class or a friend, it's important that you come up with a schedule or plan for how to keep everything neat and tidy. Without this, your locker has the potential to get

messy and out of hand, especially when nobody takes responsibility for the mess!

OPTIMAL ORGANIZATION FOR TWEENS

I *KNOW HOW HARD BEING* a tween can be. No matter how you look at it, you're facing a huge number of changes as well as new and exciting experiences. When you're first learning to get organized and keep everything separate, it may seem overwhelming. The most important thing you can do is to remember that there are many ways to stay organized, and many of them can involve fun and creativity. Just remember, you're optimally organizing the following:

✓ Your **homework**. Find or create and keep a clean, uncluttered space in which you can focus on your homework and have everything you need at hand. Keep a schedule of what's due when.

✓ Your **backpack**. Make sure your backpack isn't hurting your back. If it is, get one that works better or figure out how to put less into it. Keep it neat and clean by giving it more frequent attention, at least on a weekly basis.

✓ Your **binder(s)**. Try a thin binder for each subject. If you use just one binder, make sure it has plenty of storage options. No loose papers! And use color-coded dividers for each subject.

✓ Your **locker**. If you're sharing, come up with a plan for also sharing the responsibility of keeping it neat and tidy. Get whatever products or add-ons will help you keep your locker well organized. Never just throw stuff in!

CHAPTER 2: FIND TIME FOR FUN TIME

As a GROWING YOUNG PERSON, sometimes it feels as though you have so many things you want to do but not enough time to do them all. School is becoming even more challenging than you thought it would be with all the assignments, tests, and quizzes, which keep you constantly busy, both at school and at home. It can feel as if schoolwork is taking up most of your free time! Don't get me wrong, school *is* important, but you also need time for other activities. Sports, extracurricular clubs, and hanging out with friends are things you want to fit in your schedule. Parents understand how you sometimes feel overwhelmed, and they can help you figure out solutions. If you feel as though you're under a lot of stress and don't know if it's because of your schedule, here's a quick quiz to assess whether or not it's time to have a talk with your parents.

QUIZ: ARE YOU FEELING OVERWHELMED?

IF YOU ARE IN GRADES 4–7, this quiz is for you! It will help you understand exactly how your work is affecting your ability to relax and not be stressed out. Even though it's always important to do your homework and study, other things are just as important. Consider the following questions, circling your answer to each one:

Do you spend a big chunk of the day after school working on homework?

☐ Yes

☐ No

☐ Sometimes

☐ Rarely

Do you get angry easily when you're having trouble with homework?

☐ Yes

☐ No

☐ Sometimes

☐ Rarely

When you get home after a long day, do you have time to relax?

☐ Yes

☐ No

☐ Sometimes

☐ Rarely

Do your parents ask you to spend all evening studying?

☐ Yes

☐ No

☐ Sometimes

☐ Only when there's an important test

Do you think school is really important?

☐ Yes

☐ No

☐ Sometimes

☐ Rarely

When you're at school, do you feel as if you're always falling further behind?

☐ Yes

☐ No

☐ Sometimes

☐ Rarely

When you're at school, do you feel as if you're ahead of the rest of the class?

☐ Yes

☐ No

☐ Sometimes

☐ Rarely

WHAT THE ANSWERS MEAN

*Do you spend a big chunk of the day
after school working on homework?*

If you answered yes to this question, it may be a good time to switch up your routine. Talk to your parents about changing your homework schedule and finding time for other things after school. Sometimes parents think homework is quick and easy, so they may not understand what you mean when you ask. Always be sure to talk to your parents if you have too much going on after school and not enough fun time!

*Do you get angry easily when you're
having trouble with homework?*

If you answered yes to this question, you may be having trouble focusing on your schoolwork. Maybe it's because you work too hard during the day, or you're not eating enough of the right foods. But in the end, it comes down to whether or not you're finding the work difficult. If you're constantly doing homework and still have trouble keeping up with the workload, talking to your parents or teachers about the amount of work you've been doing is an important first step!

*When you get home after a long day,
do you have time to relax?*

If you answered no to this question, it's time to change your approach to homework. Talk to your parents about a more flexible schedule that allows you to switch up the type of work you do during the day and have some time to relax. If they don't think this is a good idea, suggest a schedule that lets you relax and also get your homework done. They will appreciate your effort at making your own plan and goals. It's important to consider all sides of the story!

*Do your parents ask you to spend
all evening studying?*

If you answered yes to this question, maybe it's time to take the same action as in the previous question. Even though school is very important during this time in your life, finding time for activities and hanging out with friends can actually help you keep a clear head. Talk to your parents and teachers about other ways you can make sure you're studying properly. If you have a big test or assignment coming up, find the right amount of time to prepare for it.

Do you think school is really important?

If you answered no to this question, it may be because you're having a hard time with stress and need a new approach to doing homework. School is an important part of anybody's life, so making sure it stays important in your eyes will affect your future. But don't think about the future too much—this is the perfect time for you to be involved in activities and to make the most of having fun.

When you're at school, do you feel as if you're always falling further behind?

If you answered yes to this question, talking to your teacher about other ways you can study is very important. Just because you feel as though you're falling behind doesn't mean that you can't fix it. Talking to your parents can also help fix your problems. Don't worry about them getting mad at you. Everybody falls behind sometimes.

When you're at school, do you feel as if you're ahead of the rest of the class?

If you answered yes to this question, that's not necessarily a bad thing! You may be feeling confident because you're getting ahead of the group, but you also may be getting *too* far ahead. It's important to learn as a group so you can help each other along. You might also be doing too much homework ahead of time. Talk to your parents about adjusting your routine so you can work *with* your classmates.

I was involved in a *lot* of activities in school when I was your age. I said yes to almost everything that came my way because I thought it was all so exciting. I wanted to do it all! After a while, though, trying to do it all became very stressful. I found myself worrying about how I was going to get my schoolwork done and still be in this play or that club or become an all-star softball player or spend time with my friends. It made everything less fun. I finally talked to my parents about it, and we figured some things out that helped. Some of what I learned is right here in this book!

TWEEN TIME BALANCE TIPS

TIME MANAGEMENT IS A VERY important skill that everyone needs to practice in order to be successful. As a young person, you're still growing into your habits. This is why it's important to start learning and practicing good time-management habits that will help you be less stressed and give you more time for everything you need and want to do. By following these helpful hints designed for young people like you, you'll get all kinds of happy results!

✓ Remember to **clean up after yourself** at the end of each day. This will save you from having to do a huge amount of cleaning on weekends. Pick up things like dishes, clothes, and papers in your room. This shows initiative and helps your parents see that you are growing into a responsible person.

✓ Writing **to-do lists** will help you stay organized when you have a lot going on. If you're balancing school, sports, and/or other hobbies, you've got a lot going on! Making plans with friends is also in the mix. When you have chores to do on top of all that, you have a recipe for potential disaster. Making a to-do list and putting the most important things at the top will help you get through the big stuff first.

✓ You have to **learn to say no** when you're feeling stressed or tired. Just because you have practice for your team scheduled for 8 p.m. every night doesn't mean you can't miss it once in a while. You feel as though you always have to go, but if you run yourself down, you could get sick or become way too stressed. Always tell your parents how you feel. You have to be honest and clear or else they won't understand.

✓ **Find time to take breaks** during your busy schedule. When you're making a to-do list for your week, make sure you put down time to hang out with friends! The weekend is a great time to do that. Talk to your parents about having a free night that you can use for fun activities you like doing.

✓ **Pick something to do that you enjoy**. If you're currently involved in an activity outside of school that you don't really like, talk to your parents about changing it. You shouldn't be doing something you don't like to do! I know you may feel as if you're letting your parents down because they want you to do it, but parents are there to *support* you and *encourage* you to do the things *you* love. Always be honest and open with your parents because they're your strongest supporter!

✓ **Find out what you like to do**. If you're stuck on choosing something you can enjoy both inside and outside of school, try out a bunch of different things to see what works for you. Try things you've never tried before—even things you think you wouldn't be good at. You may be surprised to find something really cool to do. This will also help you balance your time because, in the process, you'll figure out what's *not* working. Never sacrifice something you like just because it conflicts with your homework or chores. Talk to your parents about a new schedule so you can do stuff you really want to do!

✓ **Breathe!** Just stop and take a deep breath. Remember that what you didn't finish today, you can always finish tomorrow. When you have so much stuff to finish and it's the end of the day, it can really send you into panic mode. I'm here to tell you that it's *more* important to sit down for five minutes, take a few deep breaths, and remember there's always tomorrow. Just because it feels as if something has to be finished now doesn't mean you can't take care of it the next day if you're feeling overwhelmed.

✓ **Remember that you have a support system**. Your family and friends are there for you. If you have a big assignment coming up and you feel pressed for time, turn to your parents or siblings for help. If you have a big test approaching and you're worrying about the amount of time you've spent studying, talk to your friends about forming study buddy circles where you can help each other out with preparing.

HOW TO: LISTING THINGS OUT FOR BALANCE

IF YOU'RE STRESSED DURING THE day and find it hard to make time for different kinds of activities, making a list that balances your work and school is a very important skill to learn. Below, we will focus on making the best possible list and customizing it so the process becomes fun and exciting to do at the beginning of every week. Following these few steps and examples will help you a lot!

SCHOOLWORK AND SPORTS EVENTS

As our first example, fill in the following list with the types of things you do daily during each week. This will give you a good idea about how you can manage your time in between. Examples include sports, tests, assignments, and homework.

Monday:

_____

Tuesday:

_____

Wednesday:

_____

Thursday:

_____

Friday:

_____

CHORES AT HOME

If you've listed a few things for each day, you've already got a very busy schedule. However, by making a full list that outlines what you have to do each day, the jobs will feel so much easier. Practice filling out this next list, which will help you keep track of the chores you have to do each day.

WEEKLY CHORES:

Examples: Clean my room, do the dishes, walk the dog (Fill in the spaces with your own list.)

Monday:

_____

Tuesday:

_____

Wednesday:

_____

Thursday:

_____

Friday:

_____

Saturday:

_____

Sunday:

_____

ACTIVITIES AND FRIENDS

Another great list to make is a list of all the things you want to do that *aren't* chores or schoolwork. By listing these for each day, you can plan to include them into your master schedule.

Who do you want to hang out with this week?

_____

_____

_____

_____

What types of sports or other activities do you want to accomplish by the end of the week?

_____

_____

_____

_____

What other goals or special projects do you want to do by the end of the week?

_____

_____

_____

_____

I was walking a group of kids through this exercise once, and when we got to the part about the non-school and non-chore activities, I gave them some time to list the things they wanted to do next week. After a few minutes, I asked, "Okay, is everyone done?" Everyone was done except for one little girl who said she needed more time. After another minute I asked again, but she *still* wasn't done. When she finally finished, she had a list of things that was three times as long as the other two lists *combined*. I don't know if she was very popular or just wanted to do a lot of things, but she pretty quickly realized she wouldn't be able to do all those on top of the things she had to do for school and home. Sometimes you just need a reality check!

HOW TO: WORKING UP A WEEKLY SCHEDULE

A list will only work if you're willing to give everything on it a try. If you're not committed to sticking to your list, it probably won't work. Although making a list may seem like a lot of work at the beginning of the week, it will *save* you time in the end. It will also show your parents and teachers that you care about getting things done. By preparing yourself for everything you have to do during the week, you can plan your time and make sure you get some fun time in as well. The skill of planning and managing your time is one that will serve you well as you advance to the higher grades in school. When you get to high school, you'll be focused on getting a job, and life will be moving much more quickly than you ever thought possible. This is why it's very important to establish time-management skills while you can. But that doesn't mean it can't be fun, too!

You can make your weekly list look as awesome as you want. Make it fun and exciting to create your list for each week by using different pieces of colored paper and creating templates for each week. You can also use different colored pencils, markers, and decorations to make your list super cool.

QUIZ: THE WEEKLY ROUTINE

If you find yourself under a lot of stress or you're not enjoying the chores and other things you have to do each week, consider changing your schedule. Even though it might seem hard sometimes, there are ways to figure out whether you need to talk to your parents about a change. Stress is not good, especially at your age! Answer the following questions in order to talk to your parents about whether or not you need a change in your routine or weekly activities.

Do you have enough time to hang out with your friends during your weekly routine?

- ☐ Yes
- ☐ No
- ☐ Sometimes
- ☐ Rarely
- ☐ Only when my homework is done

Do you feel stressed or unwell when you've had a full day of activities?

- ☐ Yes
- ☐ No
- ☐ Sometimes
- ☐ Rarely

Do you feel sad or anxious during the week when you're super busy?

- ☐ Yes
- ☐ No
- ☐ Sometimes
- ☐ Rarely

WHAT THE ANSWERS MEAN

Do you have enough time to hang out with your friends during your weekly routine?

Even though sports and other activities are important parts of a healthy routine, you also need to take time to hang out with your friends and be a part of social activities. You might have friends at sports events or other activities, but the friends you don't see during these events are equally important. Because of the stress of a busy routine, you may not find the time to hang out with the people you really want to spend time with. To make sure you keep your friends and have balance, talk to your parents about finding time to fit in activities with your friends. Even though you might have a lot going on, parents can help you fit in other things, but you have to tell them! Never be afraid to go to them and ask if you can make a change once a week so you can hang out with a friend. However, don't spring these plans on them at the last minute. If you've already made a commitment to something you like to do, your parents will expect you to follow through with it. That doesn't mean they'll always expect it, but you do need to be responsible.

Do you feel stressed or unwell when you've had a full day of activities?

If your weekly routine is packed full of different things to do before and/or after school, after a while it may feel like too much. You need to think about the amount of free time you have during the week and how too many activities could be hurting you. You're probably trying to do too much if you feel any of the following during the week: stress, anxiety, tiredness, inability to focus during school, or difficulty concentrating when you try to work on different tasks or assignments. Any of these is a sure sign that you need to slow down and refocus your attention on having less stress in your life!

Do you feel sad or anxious during the week when you're super busy?

Another sign that your schedule may be too packed is if you're feeling sad that you have to do different activities. If you're experiencing feelings of sadness or regret while participating in your weekly routine, always be sure to talk to your parents or teachers about it. This is very important. Being sad about having to do things is not good. By being open and communicating with other people in your life, you can help change your routine and bring yourself contentment and relaxation.

FINAL THOUGHTS ON TIME MANAGEMENT

IT'S INCREDIBLY IMPORTANT FOR YOU to find time to do all the things you want to do. Yes, sports and other activities are a great way to stay involved and be active, but that's not the most important part of managing your time. You need to stay on top of schoolwork, participate in activities, and find time to hang out with friends and be a part of family moments. The idea of time management can be stressful for anyone, but managing your time will save you stress and the energy you'll need to focus on things that are fun at the end of the week. Here are a few final tips for developing great time-management skills:

✓ Talk to your parents about managing your time so you can find more room in your schedule to hang out with your friends, play video games, or work on a special project. Parents are always very open to how you feel and think. Don't ever be afraid of talking to someone just because the idea of disappointing him or her scares you.

✓ Make to-do lists and charts. Trust me, you'll be able to focus much more efficiently if you're able to create things that will keep you focused. This will also help you plan for free time that you may not feel as though you have now.

✓ Finally, remember to *breathe*! If you've made the perfect schedule that fits in all these categories, great. But you have to remember that too many activities can leave you tired or sick. Take a few moments now and then to just breathe and remember that not everything has to be done in one day!

Have you ever heard the phrase *Rome wasn't built in a day*? Well, it's true! You can't do absolutely *everything*. Sometimes you do have to choose a few things to just let go of. Although that may feel bad at first, the extra breathing room in your schedule will feel really good!

CHAPTER 3: HOMEWORK HELP

OKAY, SO NOW IT'S TIME to really get down to the nitty-gritty of one area that many tweens struggle with, which is *homework*. It feels like a drag to do it, especially when you get home from school and want to be doing just about anything *other* than more schoolwork! Homework is one of those things in life you just have to deal with. But fear not! Help is on the way ... *homework help*, to be specific. This chapter is going to be the one that sends you over the top when it comes to getting your homework done and having the time you want for other things.

Making sure you can get your homework completed on time and correctly can seem like a nearly impossible task. There are lots of assignments to keep track of and projects you have to plan for. Here's a plan that will help you stay ahead of everything you need to do. If you follow this plan, you'll be able to do the following:

✓ Get your homework done fast and have time for things you want to do at home.

✓ Get your homework done well and get better grades.

✓ Get projects done in a timely way so there is no last-minute rush, which can be really stressful.

✓ Always have your homework with you, so you won't ever spend the time doing it only to leave it at home or on the bus by accident.

It may sound funny that you need to plan and put together a homework space and *Homework Helper Tool Kit* to stay on top of things, but it really does help. When you take the time to get everything you need in order, here's what will happen:

✓ You won't waste time looking for things.

✓ You will always have what you need.

✓ You will always be able to get assignments done the way you're supposed to.

Homework is a really important part of your life. It's how you make sure you remember what you have learned in school. Something that many people forget about homework is that the better you are at doing it, the better you are at taking tests. Making sure all your homework is done and done right means you will have the best study tools to prepare for a test. After all, if a teacher thinks something is important enough to send home as homework, you can bet it will be on a test, too!

So let's get started.

TRACK WHAT YOU NEED TO DO

YOU WILL NEED THE FOLLOWING:

✓ A pen or pencil

✓ A homework planner book

✓ A calendar or whiteboard with the days on it (and whiteboard pens) *Remember making the DIY dry-erase board/poster board calendar

Your school or your teacher may have given you a special homework planner to use. Sometimes it's the same notebook you use for the class. You need to know how the teacher wants you to use this notebook first.

Answer these questions:

✓ Does your teacher want you to have a parent sign the book every night?

✓ Does your teacher want you to write down the assignments in the book every day?

If you answered yes to either or both questions, those are the things you need to make sure to do. When you come home, rewrite the assignments on your creatively designed DIY calendar or whiteboard. If you didn't make one of those, tape up a piece of paper and use that for your calendar. Writing what you have to do several times will help you remember it!

But where are you going to put these notes about what you have to do? You're going to put them in the special area you're going to create where you will do your homework.

FIND THE BEST PLACE TO DO HOMEWORK

WHILE YOU MAY THINK YOU can do your homework anywhere—on the bus, in the car, on the couch— you really can't. Homework needs to be done in an area that is set aside for just that purpose. Why? The human brain is a very funny

I AM YOUR BRAIN!

61

thing. Besides being like a big, squishy sponge, it knows what it is supposed to be ready to do by the clues we give it. This is why putting on pajamas before you go to bed is important. When the brain sees the pajamas come out, it says to itself, "Oh yeah, now it's time to slow down and get sleepy!" That's the way the brain is—it needs clues and reminders to get ready for what it has to do next.

Remember the DIY homework organization kit you created. Here's where you'll keep it and use it. Make an area to do your homework that your brain is going to recognize and say to itself, "Oh yeah, time to pay attention and do homework." This means your brain will work faster for you so you get your homework done because it knows that is what you want from it!

Having a special homework area also means you won't lose stuff and will have everything you need in one spot. To get a homework area together, you'll need the following:

✓ A place to sit

✓ A desktop or table to work on

✓ A basket or box to hold the things you need

✓ Your calendar or homework book

✓ A timer or clock

Once you have all of that together, you want to look around your homework space. Make sure it isn't *busy*. A *busy* space is one with a lot of pictures or other types of distractions in it—like a TV or a radio. You want those to be somewhere else so you can stay focused and get your homework done fast so you can then move on to other things.

When I was a teacher, I remember one of my students having a really hard time getting his homework done on time and done well. We finally sat down one day, and I asked him about the place where he actually did his homework. As it turned out, the student was trying to do his homework in the lobby of the very busy apartment building where he lived while waiting for his mother to get home from work and unlock the apartment. The chair was comfy, but he had no desk or anything to spread out on. He had to try and hold everything in his lap, which just wasn't working very well. When I had a parent-teacher meeting with his mother, we talked about how he needed a better space to do his homework. It was decided that he was old enough to carry a key and let himself into the apartment, where he could do his homework at his desk. Things went a LOT better for him after that!

Once you have your homework spot together, it's time to gather all the things you need to do your homework.

GET EVERYTHING YOU NEED IN ONE SPOT

NOW THAT YOU HAVE IDENTIFIED a good homework area, it's time to gather together everything you need in one spot. The best way to do this is to make a *Homework Helper Tool Kit*. This can be a basket, a bag, or even a drawer in the area you are working in. It just has to be a place where you can keep all the things you need to get your homework done.

Think about it—there's nothing worse than trying to get your homework done so you can go on to do other things but then spending half the evening searching for the books and tools you need. Putting together a *Homework Helper Tool Kit* helps you always have the right things, right *when* you need them, right *where* you need them.

MAKE A HOMEWORK HELPER TOOL KIT

THE FIRST THING TO DO is to decide what you're going to keep things in. A box or basket usually works best, especially one that has a lid. It's also a good idea to have a few smaller boxes you can fit inside your tool kit because this will help keep things organized inside it. Here is what you should have:

✓ Plain paper (with no lines)

✓ Crayons or markers

✓ Glue and scissors

✓ A few report covers

✓ Lined paper

✓ Graph paper

✓ Tape

✓ An eraser (or two or three!)

✓ A dictionary

✓ A thesaurus

✓ Pencils and a sharpener

✓ Blue or black pens

✓ A highlighter

Here's a trick that will help you make sure to always do your homework in the right color. Make a list of all your classes and all your teachers. Write down next to their names what type of paper they want their homework done on (lines, graph, or plain), what color ink or pencil they want it done in, and what they want on all your homework (name, class, grade, period, and so on). This way, you know that the homework will be turned in the way each one wants it. Tape this list to the inside of your *Homework Helper Tool Kit* and check it each time *before* you start so you make sure you are doing things right. Sometimes it can be helpful to have the supplies separated by class and teacher, too.

TIMER OR CLOCK

You'll also need a timer or clock for your homework area. A good timer or clock is not a *luxury*, it's a *necessity*. It will serve you like an alarm clock. You can use a regular clock, but an official timer or the stopwatch setting on a cell phone is ideal. When you start your homework, you want to set the timer so you work for 45 minutes and then take a 10- or 15-minute break before going back to work if you haven't finished everything.

Talk with your mom and dad, and ask them to help you set up the timer. It may be better for you to only work for 30 minutes and then have a break. By using a timer, you'll focus more on getting your homework done faster. By taking a break, you'll make sure you never get too tired when doing your homework.

The other cool thing about using a clock is that you can then start having fun getting your homework done by playing your own version of *beat the clock*. For example, you might challenge yourself to finish the next page of your spelling homework in seven minutes or less—and you'll have the timer to see if you can do it!

HOW TO TAKE BREAKS DURING HOMEWORK

WHEN YOU TAKE A HOMEWORK break, it's important that it's just long enough to give you a little rest, but not so long that you get distracted by other things. Ten or fifteen minutes is usually the best amount of time. During a break, you should get up and walk around, have a snack, or just take a few minutes to do something else.

One of the best breaks to take is a *music* break. Listen to a song you like, have a glass of water, and then start the timer again so you can get back to work.

The worst kind of break to take is one where you try to watch something on TV. The reason that a music break is better is that songs are way shorter than shows. It's much harder to stop watching TV and get back to homework than it is to listen to a full song or two and then get back to work. This is why coming up with a plan about when you'll do your homework is important, too. If you plan *when* you do your homework, you won't miss out on the other things you want to do!

LET'S MAKE A PLAN!

OKAY, TIME TO MAKE A plan. You need to know how much time you usually need to get your homework done. An hour? Two hours? Sometimes it will be longer, and sometimes it will be shorter. It really depends on how much and what kind of homework you have.

The best time to do homework is right after you get home from school. I know you may think that sounds like the *worst* time to do it because you just spent all day at school, but think about it: Right when you get home from school ...

✓ You are still in school mode, so it's easier to do school-type stuff.

✓ If you do your homework first, you won't have to stop doing something you love to do it.

But don't just walk in the door and start right away. Take some time to put together a homework schedule so you don't get exhausted by it all too soon.

SCHEDULE

THE RIGHT KIND OF HOMEWORK schedule is the one in which you also know everything else you want and need to get done that night. Your homework schedule should look something like this:

✓ Arrive home

✓ 15-minute snack and relax

✓ Get homework ready

✓ Set timer to work and begin

✓ Take 10-minute break

✓ Finish homework (repeat work/break until done)

✓ Clean up

✓ Dinner

✓ Free time

✓ Get ready for tomorrow

✓ Get ready for bed

✓ Sleepy time!

Your schedule may look a little different each day, but you get the basic idea. The more you can plan out how you need to spend your time, the more you'll get done and the more free time you'll have.

Erainna Winnett, Ed. S.

TOP SECRET TIP! THE POWER OF THE SNACK

HAVING A SNACK WHEN YOU first get home, and especially *before* you start your homework, is more important than you may think. Even if you aren't hungry, you should have a small bowl of cereal, some fruit, or a handful of nuts. Why? Because by the time you get home, it's been a long time since lunch, and it will still be a long time before dinner. Your body doesn't just need food so it has fuel for running around—your *brain* needs food so it can *think clearly*. We have to eat snacks to keep enough fuel in our bodies so we can move *and* think well.

Right when you get home is just about when you're starting to run low on fuel. You want to give your brain a little boost to help you get through your homework fast. When you take breaks during your homework, you may want to have a glass of water or a piece of fruit, too. This can help stop you from feeling tired halfway through. Just don't eat so much that you spoil your appetite for dinner! Also, make it decent, healthy food (fresh fruit, vegetables, nuts, whole grain crackers). Too many tweens are becoming overweight from eating too much junk food.

HOW TO GET STARTED

THE BEST WAY TO GET started is to use the checklist at the end of this chapter to help you plan out your homework time. You can copy it and use it every day. It can help you get started and stay on track to get everything done.

Do you remember the Christmas song that says Santa is *making a list and checking it twice*? That's what you can do, too! Of course, a list of what you need to do for homework is not nearly as much fun as a list of Christmas presents, but hey, that's life! Hang in there and you'll be able to get it done.

KNOWING WHEN TO ASK FOR HELP

ONCE YOU GET STARTED WITH your homework, you may find that you need help with some parts of it. There are many people you can ask for help with your homework, like your parents or an older brother or sister. Some schools now have after-school tutors or homework help sites where you can go online to ask for help.

The important thing about asking for help is to make sure you've tried to do it yourself first. Always look back in your notes or textbook at the lesson the homework is based on *before* you ask someone for help. Chances are, what you need is right there! When you're done with your homework, have someone check it over to make sure you have completed everything.

HAVE YOUR WORK CHECKED BY SOMEONE

THE FIRST PERSON WHO SHOULD check over your work is *you!* Stand up and stretch your arms and legs when you're done with the assignment and then sit down and look over what you have done. Make this checklist a habit when you go over your own homework:

✓ **Is every question answered?**

    YES   NO

✓ **Is my handwriting clear?**

    YES   NO

✓ **Did I answer every part of the question or assignment?**

    YES   NO

✓ **Can I find my answers on the page easily?**

    YES   NO

✓ **Did I do my homework in the correct color pen or pencil?**

    YES   NO

✓ **Are there any additional questions on the back?**

YES   NO

Except for the last question, if you answered *no* to any of the rest, go back and finish the assignment. Once this is done, have someone else check your work to make sure you haven't missed anything.

If your school or teacher requires it, have a parent sign your homework or schedule book so the teacher knows a parent checked your work.

GETTING EVERYTHING READY FOR SCHOOL

BEFORE YOU START GETTING EVERYTHING ready so you can find it for the next day, you want to read through any handouts the teacher has given or check your online class schedule if you have one to make sure there aren't any notes about things you may need for the next day. A lot of schools are now posting their assignments to their classroom pages, so you always want to make sure to check that each night. Once you are sure that you've done everything you need to do for the next day, it's time to get everything together.

One of the worst feelings in the world is to have spent a lot of time on a project or homework assignment, only to leave it at home the day it is due! Actually, there is another feeling that might even be worse: to have brought everything with you but then leave it on the bus or in the car when you were dropped off. That's even worse than leaving your lunch at home!

The best way to avoid those situations is to have a special place by the door where you put everything you need for school. Make sure that everything is in some kind of bag or box so it's easy to carry and keep together. Don't try to carry loose pieces of paper! They almost always end up getting lost. If you carry a lunch with you, put a reminder on your lunch box or bag so you don't forget. It can be as simple as a sticky note or as funny as a squeaky dog toy in the shape of a banana!

The goal is whatever helps you remember.

You also want to make sure that if your school or teacher requires you to have a homework or schedule book signed each night; that it's signed and placed in the front of your backpack or book bag. Another good habit to get into is to make sure that everything else you need for the next day is also ready. This includes gym stuff, after-school activity supplies, and any team sports stuff you may need. Oh, yes, and clothes. It's always a good idea to pick out what you are going to wear the next day *before* you go to bed!

Let's make a list of what to do by doing an exercise that involves finishing a sentence to make all of this easier:

* Every night I will put all of my school things together in _____ by the _____.

* I need to make sure that I always have _____ _____ with me to be ready for school.

* I am going to use _____ to remind me to make sure I have everything I need.

* I need _____ for after school _____ on these days: _____.

* Every night, I will pick out my _____ for the next day and put them _____.

DOUBLE-CHECK WHAT YOU NEED

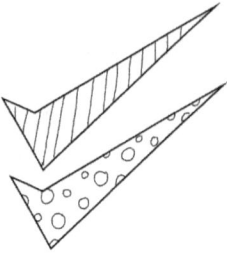

The first few times you go to do this, you may miss a few things, but that's okay. It can take a while to get into the habit of making sure you have everything you need!

ASK ABOUT EXTRA CREDIT!

EVERYONE KNOWS THAT IF YOU do a little extra work, you can often get extra credit that really helps your grade. You can ask your teacher if there's anything you can do to earn some extra credit so you can get the best grades possible. Sometimes you can give your teacher ideas about what you can do if he or she doesn't have extra credit assignments ready. Here are three great ones:

Draw a scene from the book you did a book report on.

1. Do three extra word problems in math.

2. Define 10 new words and use each one in a sentence.

If you sit and think about all the things you're learning in school and what your teachers are like, what do *you* think are three ideas for extra credit assignments that they might approve? Write them in the spaces below:

1. _____

2. _____

3. _____

Just Make Sure You Have Time. Before you ask for extra credit to raise your grade, try setting aside more time to do your homework so it's more complete. While extra credit can help you bring up your grade, it does require more time. If most of your time is spent with after-school activities or sports, adding extra credit work may not be a good idea. Instead, put more effort into the homework time you have and raise your grade that way.

THREE IMPORTANT THINGS TO REMEMBER

So NOW YOU HAVE LEARNED a whole lot about how to make sure you get your homework done fast and done right. Homework is one of the most important things about being in school. It is where you get a chance to practice what you have learned and do it yourself. It's a way of checking to be sure you understand the lesson and you won't have to worry about taking tests or exams. Here are three important things to remember about homework:

1. *Homework is about helping you.* Homework isn't something your teachers dreamed up to make your life miserable. It has a real purpose. Just like when you are learning something new in a sport, you have to practice it after someone has shown you how to do it so that *you* can do it. Some things take a lot of practice before you really get how to do them well. Homework is the same type of practice, just for different types of learning.

2. *Don't ever think there is something you don't need to know.* When I was a kid, I complained that I didn't need to know math because there were calculators. I thought when I was grown up I was never going to do math. Surprise! Everything I love to do has *something* to do with math. Sports require math. Music requires a ton of math, and so does art. Don't ever think there is something that you don't need to bother doing a good job of learning! You never know what you will need to know when you want to get really good at something. Better to get all this learning out of the way and done right at this stage in your life so you don't have to go back later when you are older. Can you imagine what it would be like now at your age to have to sit in with all the first graders to learn how to write the alphabet or your numbers? If you hadn't done the work to learn those things back when you were in first grade, you just might have to go back at some point and learn them. Think of every homework assignment as a key to a treasure chest. You just have to get the treasure map to find the chest!

3. Don't ever think there is something you can't learn. Even if you have a learning disability, there are all sorts of tips and other things that can help you learn. Some people learn things faster than others. Some people can learn by writing out the steps, and others just sort of see how things work in their mind. Everyone learns in a different way. If you wind up having a really difficult time with some homework, ask for help. You'll be surprised who would really like to help you and how much of a difference their help can make if you ask. Just say, "I am having trouble with this. Can you help me?" It's totally okay to ask for help!

GETTING READY FOR HOMEWORK SUCCESS

IF YOU THINK ABOUT ALL the things you have learned to help you do your homework better, what two things are going to be the hardest for you to do?

1. _____

2. _____

Now, think about each of them and write down how you can make it easier to do those two things. Make sure to also write down who you will ask to help you. If making a place to do your homework will be hard, you can ask your mom or dad to help you set up an area.

1. _____

2. _____

The last thing you need to do is to make a list of the people you can ask to help you with your homework and who you can ask to help you by checking your homework. They don't have to be geniuses at the subjects you are studying. If people already went through the grade you are in, chances are they can help you. After all, you don't want people who are going to just give you the answers—you want people who are going to help you discover how to find the answers on your own. Who will they be?

1. _____

2. _____

3. _____

If you put all these steps into action, you'll do better at finishing your homework on time and getting good grades!

THE CHECKLIST

Date: _____

Today I need to: _____

I have homework in these classes:

_____

I will start my homework at _____.

I will work for _____ minutes and take a _____ minute break.

For a snack, I will have _____.

During break, I will _____.

When I am done, _____ will check my work.

Now check these off as you finish them:

____ Homework done

____ Homework checked

____ Homework packed and ready for tomorrow

____ Homework book signed

CHAPTER 4: STUDY SKILLS FOR YOU

I KNOW FROM YEARS OF working with kids your age that it's hard to really figure out *how* to study, especially if you're not the best at it to begin with. That's okay! There are lots of ways to learn how to study, and we're going to take a look at them in a little more detail in this chapter. When we're finished, you'll have a whole new set of ideas that you can use to help you study, and you'll feel as though you are much better at it than you were before.

Over the years working with kids your age, I've shared all the tips that you're going to read in this chapter. But I only shared them one at a time—one here with this kid, one there with that kid. This is the first time I've gathered all the study tips together in one place and shared all of them at the same time. When you're finished learning about all the tips in this chapter, you're going to be like a superhero of studying!

FIRST THINGS FIRST

FIRST OFF, YOU MAY BE having a hard time switching between having one teacher and having several different teachers with different personalities and ways of teaching. The point of this chapter is to help you learn *flexibility* in studying because each class might call for a different approach to studying. The ways you study are going to depend on a lot of different things, including the following:

✓ **How you like to learn.** Everyone learns differently! And that's okay—we're all unique and special, and the things we do are going to be different. That means our brains are wired differently, and no two people are going to learn the same. Because of that, you may have to try some of these ideas out for yourself before you decide which ones work best for you.

✓ **How your teachers teach.** Teachers play a big role in our lives, don't they? And all of them are different, just as we are! If one of your teachers teaches in a way that you don't quite understand, you may need a little extra help in order to succeed, and that's just fine! The differences in how your teachers teach will make a difference in how *you* study.

✓ **The subject you're studying.** This is the last thing you have to think about. You're going to study differently for math than you are for science, and you'll study for language arts differently than you would for music class. Some study skills and tips will work really well for some subjects but just aren't good for others because of how the subject is structured. Like I said above, you just have to try them out and see which ones help *you* the most!

Keep the above points in mind. Don't get discouraged or frustrated! In the rest of this chapter, I'll give you a lot of tips that you can use in order to study to the best of your ability. Check them out, try them for yourself, and see what you can do with them.

QUESTIONS TO THINK ABOUT

✓ Do you learn better with pictures, by reading, or when you can apply the things you're learning?

✓ The next time you're in school, sit down and pay attention to how your different teachers teach. It'll help you figure out how you can learn from them.

✓ What's your favorite subject? Why is it your favorite subject? That may give you some hints as to how you learn best.

TIPS AND SKILLS

STUDENTS WITH BETTER STUDY SKILLS score higher on their tests. You knew that, right? These students know how to adapt their skills, how to memorize different items, and how to learn in a way that can help them apply their knowledge to any quiz or test. As I said above, everyone is different, so you'll have to try out a bunch of different things before you find the ones that work for you. Here are some of the best studying tips you can try:

It's best to take a look at your notes right after class, when it's still fresh in your memory. Why? Because you'll be doing something known as *reinforcement*. That means you're sticking something in your mind and keeping it there by repeating it. The next time you're done with a class, look at your notes before you start the next class. You'll find that it's easier for you to remember that stuff when test time comes around.

Don't cram! One problem a lot of kids have is they try to cram right before a test. If you do this, you aren't getting all the information you need when you're looking it over at the last minute. If you know you're going to have a test or quiz, start studying a few days beforehand. That way, your brain has a better chance of hanging onto the information. Also, don't study later than the time you typically go to bed. If you do, you may fall asleep while studying or just give up and go to bed. Think about studying as soon as you get home or in the early morning before you go to school. Your mind will be more alert, and it will remember things a LOT better than if you study right before bedtime.

Take breaks and space out your study times. You want to make sure to take short breaks on a regular basis. Your brain holds all the information that you're learning, and if you don't take a break, you're not going to remember everything that you need to remember. When you space out your study times, you'll actually take in more and remember it better than if you try to cram too much in at one time. But even if you're in for a longer study session, you're going to want to get up and stretch your legs every once in a while. You can even exercise a bit during breaks, which is like recharging your brain's battery. It will also help you make sure that you're more awake so you don't fall asleep while studying.

Don't forget anything you need to study. Do you have notes for your class? Were there worksheets? Did you bring the book home so you can study from it? Were there websites that your teachers told you to check out before your test? Have everything handy so you don't have to interrupt your study time by getting up and trying to find something that you've forgotten.

List it! Make a list of everything you should have with you when you're studying. Do this for all your classes because it may be different for each class. Keep that list around when you're ready to study so you'll be able to organize *before* you sit down to study for a test or quiz.

Relax! When you're studying, you absolutely have to relax. Find a spot that is comfortable (but not *too* comfortable—you don't want to fall asleep!) and make sure it's not full of distractions. It's not a good idea to study in the living room if your whole family is making noise or watching TV. Feel free to turn on some calm music like classical pieces by Beethoven or Mozart. They can help you relax, and researchers have found that classical music can also help you remember things! Keep the music low, though, and make sure it doesn't have words—otherwise, you may find yourself singing along with songs instead of studying.

What you want to avoid when studying is feeling stress. Stress can actually make it harder for you to remember things because it makes your mind wander and wears your brain out. If you relax while you're studying, you'll be more likely to remember all the stuff you have to remember! Think about what you can do to relax while you're studying.

Start with the big idea and work your way out. Sometimes you just need to get the big ideas. Sit down with your information and make a big outline. The most important information will likely be the *big idea(s)*. You want to use them and remember them when it comes to taking the test. Learn the big idea(s) *first*, and then learn all the smaller pieces of information. That way, you'll have a clearer idea of your study goals. One of the best ways to do this is by making an outline. Here's an example of what that looks like:

BIG IDEA – The Milky Way is our galaxy.

Smaller Idea #1 – There are eight planets in our galaxy, and each planet is different.

1. Mercury – Information about Mercury

2. Venus – Information about Venus

3. Earth – Information about Earth

4. Mars – Information about Mars

5. Jupiter – Information about Jupiter

6. Saturn – Information about Saturn

7. Uranus – Information about Uranus

8. Neptune – Information about Neptune

Smaller Idea #2 – All the planets in the Milky Way revolve around the sun.

1. The sun is a star.

2. The sun is made of (list gases here).

That's just one example of how you can put everything together, and it doesn't have all the information about all of the planets. When you're done reading this chapter, sit down and make an outline of it, keeping the big ideas big and working your way down to the small details. That way, you'll have a better idea of what you're learning from this chapter!

Always Ask Questions. Sometimes it's hard to ask other people for help, but if you don't really understand something, go to your teacher, your parents, or your friends in order to get help with it. You want to make sure you understand what you're learning instead of just pretending to understand and then wondering what to do when it comes time to take a test or quiz. There are probably a number of people who can answer your questions, so go ahead and ask! No one is going to think less of you because you need help. It's good to admit that you need help so you can pass the test with flying colors.

Think about studying with others. It can be good to study with other people, at least as long as those people are serious about studying, like you are. Sometimes it can be more of a distraction for you, which could make you do worse on a test. But if you have friends who are ready to study and want to learn all the stuff you've been learning in class, go ahead and get together with them and study for the test as a group – it can really help *all* of you, especially if you learn in different ways. Some of your friends

may be strong where you are weak, and you may be strong where some of them are weak. You can all help each other do well when you work together!

You don't have to study with friends, either. Talk to your parents or a sibling who might be willing to study with you. They can sometimes give you more information that you may not know, and they may be a good study buddy that you never thought about before! Test yourself or have someone else test you on the material to figure out what your weak and strong points are. Sometimes you can take a practice test or use a worksheet in your class. Make sure to use those to test yourself as well. Other people can be a big help when you're studying, so make sure you make the most of that by getting some study buddies. Think of people you trust to study with you. Make a list of them and see if they'll help you study the next time a quiz or test comes around!

1. _____

2. _____

3. _____

4. _____

MORE QUESTIONS TO THINK ABOUT

✓ Have you ever tried any of these study tips? How did they work for you? Are there any of them that you know work for you? Make sure you try them out first, and then move on to the ones you aren't sure about.

✓ Did you ever try to cram? How did you feel? Did it work for you, or was it harder for you to perform on your test or quiz the next day?

✓ Have you ever tried studying with your friends? Did it work? Was it harder?

✓ Are there any study tips I haven't mentioned here that you already try? If they work for you, keep doing them! There's always more than what I mentioned here!

HOW TO: MEMORIZING INFORMATION

MEMORIZING CAN BE REALLY DIFFICULT, especially if you're trying to do it for a big test or something else that's really important. But there are some tips you can use in order to make sure you memorize things well. Try these out if you have a hard time memorizing stuff and see which ones help you the most!

Acronyms. What is an acronym? An acronym is a word you use in order to memorize a list or a group of ideas. Many people use acronyms because they see the main word as a *trigger* for the rest of the words, and hints help your memory kick in. If you associate an idea with a particular word, you're going to be more likely to remember it and be able to hold onto the information in the future as well.

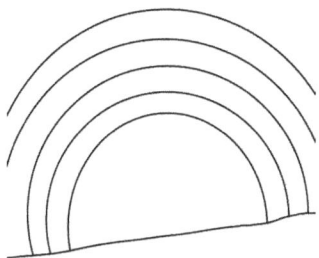

Can you tell me all the colors in a rainbow? If you're like many students, your mind likely went to "ROY-G-BIV," which is an acronym you use to remember the colors of the rainbow. Each letter of the acronym is the first letter of one of the colors of the rainbow. So what are they? **R**ed, **O**range, **Y**ellow, **G**reen, **B**lue, **I**ndigo, and **V**iolet. That's an acronym. You may have to make up your acronyms in order to use them, but that's okay—whatever helps you remember is what you should do. Try making up an acronym for this section or the previous section of this chapter so you can remember what you've learned.

_____

_____

_____

Singing and Poetry. You may think it sounds silly to sit there singing or saying a poem, but think about how many songs you know. When you ride in a car, do you know all the words to the newest pop song that comes on the radio?

How many songs can you sing along with on a car trip? For some reason, our brains remember songs *really* easily, so if you make up a song in order to learn a certain idea or set of ideas, you'll likely get it *stuck in your head* so you can use it during your test or quiz. The sillier or funnier the tune, the more easily you'll remember it.

If you're not much for singing, you can try rhyming and poetry. It works much the same way as singing—writing poems (with or without rhyming) that help you remember things. These two ideas work really well together and will help keep your thoughts straight when it comes time to remember them later on. Try making up a song or writing a poem to help you remember some of the study tips we talked about in this chapter.

_____

_____

_____

Practice with Flash Cards. One thing you'll see a lot of people do when they're trying to memorize stuff is use flash cards. They're a great way to learn vocabulary words, or they can help you with big ideas or to remember lists of items you need to memorize. Flash cards are an easy way to take studying with you when you're on the go—you can use flash cards in the car, while waiting for dinner, or even for a quick review right before your test. You also learn more while you're making them because the act of writing helps you reinforce the ideas you're learning!

The point of flash cards is to give you the big ideas (which we talked about above) so you can remember all the smaller ideas as you go. Think of them as a different way of outlining ideas, which we talked about in Tips and Skills. Want to remember all the study skills we've talked about in this chapter? Try memorizing them with flash cards! Flash cards help you remember the big ideas, which then trigger the smaller ones.

Use Images. Pictures are a lot of fun, and many people like to use them when they're learning about a new idea. Some people who prefer to use pictures over words are called *visual learners.* Visual learners learn more when you give them pictures of what's being learned instead of just talking about it. If you think you may be a visual learner, you may want to watch some YouTube videos about your subject, or make flash cards with pictures instead of (or in addition to) words. You can also look for charts or graphs that talk about the subject or ideas you're studying. Ask your

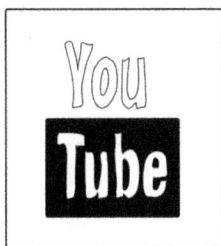

parents' permission before using the Internet, and maybe they can even help you find what you're looking for so you know you're looking at the right thing! Do you learn better with pictures? Try using pictures to summarize this chapter. Ask your parents for help if you need it—they can help you understand the material better, and they can give you ideas about how to put it in the form of pictures!

Find Patterns. Are there any patterns in what you're studying? Are there ideas or themes that seem to come up again and again? If you notice patterns and themes, they can help you remember what you're learning. Think about making sentences out of your ideas instead of just learning individual words. You could make a whole sentence about how topics are related. That way, instead of learning three different vocabulary words, you may be able to combine those three words into one sentence, which means it will take less effort to remember them. The main word can trigger your memory to remember the sentence, and then you'll remember the other words as you go. Those patterns can really help, and you'll learn a lot faster. Are there patterns in this chapter? Write them down and put them together so you can memorize them better.

_____

_____

_____

Imitation is a great way to master something. Some people do their best work when they imitate other people. This is especially true when you're learning how to do something as opposed to just memorizing ideas or topics. Some people will use this study skill when they're doing math or science. Meet with someone (a teacher, an older sibling, and so on) who knows the subject better than you do who will be able to show you what you're supposed to do with it. Then you go back and forth, watching what the other person does and copying it. If you mirror what he or she is doing and understand it step by step, you should be able to then do it on your own without having to watch every time. It will take some getting used to, but this sort of technique can be really helpful if you're someone who learns by doing instead of by just watching. The next time you aren't sure about a concept in math or another class, try out this technique for yourself.

Above all else, you need to practice. Have you ever heard the phrase *practice makes perfect*? It's true! Above everything else, you will remember best when you're actually practicing what you're doing. You may have to repeat those flash cards dozens of times, or you may have to try that math problem a few times before you get it right, but eventually, if you practice the right way, you'll really remember it when it comes time to do so.

Recite the information over and over again, and see how much it can help you in the long run.

A FEW MORE QUESTIONS TO THINK ABOUT

✓ Which of these techniques for memorizing information have you tried for yourself? Did they work? How would you try them differently?

✓ Did you learn any techniques that you hadn't heard of before reading this chapter? Are you going to try them out?

✓ Do you have your own memorizing tricks that work for you? How did you learn them?

✓ Try out at least two of these tips in the next week and see how they work for you!

If you try out all these tips, you'll find ones that work for you! Finding the right technique can really help you succeed in your classwork. It may take a bit of work for you to find the right studying and memorizing techniques, but it will be time well spent when you see your grades start to get better! Play with them, tweak them, and see what works for you and what doesn't. In the long run, you'll find that everyone has different things that work for them, and you'll be less stressed and enjoy school more when you get clear on what works best for you.

Now that you've gotten through this chapter, test what you've learned with this quiz. I hope the information in this chapter helped you learn the best ways to study!

POP QUIZ!

1. Why do different people learn differently?

_____

_____

2. Do different subjects require different ways of studying? Why?

_____

_____

3. Name four of the study methods listed in this chapter.

_____

_____

4. Why is it important to take breaks when you're studying?

_____

_____

5. Why is it important to make sure you're calm and relaxed while studying?

_____

_____

6. Why could singing and rhyming help improve your memory?

_____

_____

7. Why is practicing important?

_____

_____

POP QUIZ ANSWERS

1. Because we're all different and think differently.

2. Sometimes. Some study skills and tips will work really well for some subjects but aren't good for others because of how the subject is structured.

3. See Tips and Skills section.

4. Because our brains can only take in small amounts of information at a time. After that, we start forgetting.

5. Because it helps you concentrate and remember information better. Stress makes it harder for your brain to work well.

6. If you make up a song, poem, or rhyme to learn something, it'll get "stuck in your head," and you'll be able to use it to access information during your test or quiz.

7. You'll remember best when you are actually practicing what you're doing.

CHAPTER 5: TEST PREP TIPS

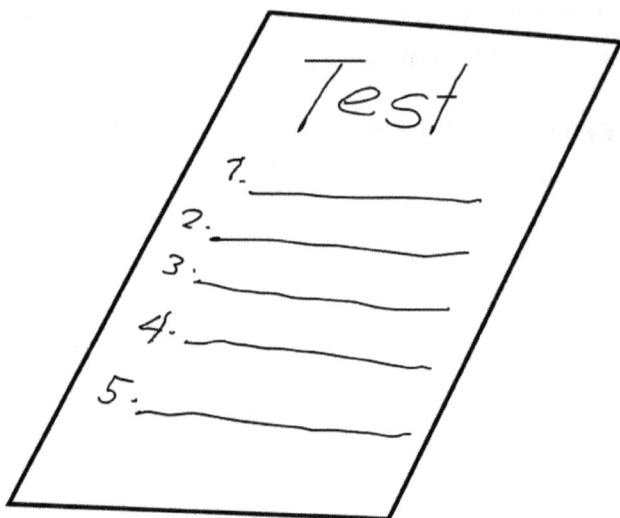

HERE'S A LITTLE NIGHTMARE SCENARIO that I've seen many tweens experience: You're feeling good because it's Friday, which means you're looking forward to the weekend. You walk into school and sit down in one of your classes, and the teacher says, "Okay, everyone, it's time to take that test I announced last week." Your heart literally skips a beat as it jumps. Test? What test? You don't remember anything about a test. How could there

be a test? You haven't studied for it *at all*. You're pretty sure this is going to go down in history as one the greatest test-taking disasters ever recorded ...

Sound familiar? If not, great! If it does sound even vaguely familiar, this chapter is going to change all that for you. If you're starting to follow any of the advice on getting organized from earlier in the book, hopefully you'll be keeping better track of things like upcoming test dates. This chapter is going to let you in on my best secrets for how to get ready for taking a test so you do as well as you can on it.

As a young student, it's very important for you to take tests seriously. Your experience in school will help shape your future. This doesn't mean you should panic when a test comes up. In fact, it's quite the opposite! Believe it or not, there's a way to make test taking fun. It may seem like a drag when you have to take tests in your different classes, but it doesn't have to be. By preparing well ahead of time and learning to reduce anxiety when it comes time for the test, you can make sure you remember as much information as possible.

There are many ways you can learn to prepare properly when it comes time to take a test, and this chapter will walk you through some key tips to achieve the best grades you can. The tips will also help you figure out your strengths and weaknesses while at the same time helping you gear up for the road ahead. Test taking in elementary or middle school can be a little scary. However, if you're able to take in everything in this chapter, you'll be able to reduce your anxiety in no time and reach for the stars. All it takes is a little initiative and motivation!

HIT THE GROUND RUNNING

WHEN YOUR TEACHER ANNOUNCES A test, write down the date and figure out how much time you have to prepare. If you have an agenda or notebook that you use to keep track of important dates, use it! If you don't have one, make a note on a nearby sheet of paper and then be sure to write it down on your calendar at home. I strongly recommend using a school planner or agenda. It will help you with your newly learned organizational skills and practically guarantees you won't have a nightmare like the one mentioned at the beginning of this chapter.

Hit the ground running is a phrase kind of like *strike while the iron is hot.* You probably don't use either of these phrases, but they mean similar things. They are both about taking immediate action without waiting. That's the most important thing when it comes to getting ready for a test. If you're one who puts things off, you simply have to change that. The whole idea is to seize the moment as soon as you find out about a test and get started preparing for it right away.

QUESTIONS TO THINK ABOUT

IF THE TEST IS IN a subject you struggle with and think you'll need additional help to prepare for, talk to your teacher when you have a chance. Let your teacher know that you're a little nervous about the test and want to have a one-on-one session with him or her. By showing that you care about your own schooling, your teachers will see how responsible you are and will help you out with whatever you need. Don't feel shy or nervous by reaching out to them—teachers are there to provide you with the support you need! As an example, let's say you're having a tough time in math and your teacher announces a test for the next week. Answer the following questions truthfully and honestly by circling your answer for each one:

Do you think you understand the material that will be covered on the test?

Yes

Maybe

Not really

I won't be able to pass

Do you struggle with any of the concepts?

Yes

Maybe

Not really

I don't understand any of the material

Would you ask your teacher for help?

Yes

Maybe

Not really

I'm pretty shy and don't want to ask for help

What about forming a study group with your classmates? Would that help?

Yes

Maybe

Not really

I don't feel comfortable in those situations

WHAT YOUR ANSWERS MEAN

Do you think you understand the material that will be covered on the test?

If you answered *yes* to this question, you're good to go! If you are truly confident that you'll be able to study for the content covered on the test without any additional help, you could be just fine. However, never be afraid to go over concepts and review key terms or ideas with a teacher or parent. Sometimes it helps to talk things over with someone to get a better understanding of the material. If you answered anything other than *yes*, your first step when you get home should be to sit down and write up a plan. We'll go over test-taking tips and how to prepare later on in this chapter.

Do you struggle with any of the concepts?

If you answered *yes* or *I don't understand any of the material*, you should follow the advice from above and make a time to meet with your teacher. You can also try talking to him or her right after the class where he or she made the announcement. To be successful on the test, you have to understand at least some of the basic concepts!

Would you ask your teacher for help?

This can be a little scary, especially if you're a very shy person. Asking for help may make you feel less smart, but in fact it's quite the opposite! Showing initiative and trying to better your chances of getting a good grade will show your teacher that you're willing to do what it takes to understand the material. When you're approaching your teacher about help, make sure to let him or her know exactly what you're struggling with so he or she can help you in very specific ways that won't overwhelm you.

What about forming a study group with your classmates? Would that help?

Even if you're not very motivated to form a study group with your classmates, you have to consider how helpful it could be to everyone, including you. By organizing something with your classmates, especially if it's a really hard subject, you can all help each other out. Try to get the teacher involved and maybe even lead the study group, or find someone who feels confident in helping everyone learn the material. Sacrifice a recess or sometime after school each day before the test in order to make sure you'll pass with flying colors. Even if you're a very shy person, this type of approach will help you get to know and learn from other students. By showing leadership skills and getting the ball rolling with a study group, you'll be benefiting both yourself and your classmates.

TEST PREP TIPS YOU
NEED TO SUCCEED

THE LEAD-UP TO THE TEST can be a very exhausting and nerve-wracking experience. Some students will choose to forget all about studying until the weekend or even the night before a big test. *Always try to avoid this approach!* By studying at the last minute, you won't be able to really absorb any of the material you've learned or ideas you've been struggling with. You won't be prepared for a test (especially one you think you'll do poorly on) if you cram all your studying into one night.

This is a great lesson moving forward because the tests will only get harder as you grow up. However, this doesn't have to scare you off from studying or doing well. These unique tips will help you in the coming days while you prepare for your test and are a great way to take a new approach to studying. After you read the tips, answer the questions that follow. I'll ask you to list a number of the ideas we just talked about, and you can create a plan that you think will help you the most. The items in **bold** in the following list are the main tips you need for making your own plan. The rest of the information provides an explanation as to why you should consider each tip as you move forward with your plan.

✓ Always make time for studying. If you have about a week to study for a test, **create a schedule on your existing calendar to budget at least thirty minutes of studying time each day.** This can be after school or during the day. It doesn't matter when you do it as long as you're able to completely absorb the concepts and form good study habits.

✓ Ask your teacher to explain any of the core concepts or ideas that will be covered on the test. Once your teacher announces an upcoming test, ask during class if he or she would be able to talk about all the different concepts on the test during a review session or in class. **Take careful notes when your teacher goes over everything that will be on the test.**

✓ **Go over any and all material that was covered in class thus far.** One useful thing to remember, even if you don't have a lot of notes for this particular test, is that staying organized and taking notes will help you be prepared for any tests in the future. If you don't have a lot of notes available to you, ask to share with a classmate or work from any past homework assignments you've done. This will help you remember things you learned earlier in the year.

✓ When you're about to take a test, **make sure you get a good night's sleep beforehand and always eat a full breakfast.** If you don't eat, your mind will wander, and if you don't sleep, you won't be able to remember all of the stuff you spent so much time studying!

✓ **Create a "summary sheet" that you can work from.** By emphasizing the core material, the hints your teacher has given out, and everything you've been able to learn about the material so far, you'll be able to create a sheet that helps you study the main ideas. Then you can expand on those main ideas in smaller sections to help keep your brain organized. This is also a great time to get creative with your summary sheets or study materials. Otherwise, it can seem like a very boring idea to study. Find ways to make it fun and exciting! Write every other sentence in a different color ink. Draw stars, cubes, or other objects beside each main point. Anything to make learning fun.

✓ **Create flash cards along with your summary sheet.** If you ask your parents to buy you a set of index cards, you can write questions on the front and answers on the back. Once you have all the potential questions written down, ask someone in your family to quiz you.

Although these are great tips any tween test-taker should follow, some of them will only work for certain people. If you're currently using other strategies to prepare yourself before a test, and they're working for you, continue using them. By thoughtfully planning out how you'll prepare for the test, you'll be able to eliminate much of the stress and anxiety that come with it. Use the spaces provided below to write out four tips you think will work best for you, whether they're listed above or ones you already use. Remember: It's not mandatory to practice all these tips at once. Try one or two, then add another tip for the next test. Your first test-taking experience using them will be very important in shaping how you take other tests in the future.

Study Tip #1:

_____

_____

Study Tip #2:

_____

_____

Study Tip #3:

_____

_____

Study Tip #4:

_____

_____

DEALING WITH TEST ANXIETY

A TEST CAN BE A scary experience for a person your age. It may feel as if each test will determine whether or not you pass or fail in *life*, but this is very far from the truth! Exams are designed to test your knowledge of the material to see if you know it. Tests aren't meant to punish you or anything like that.

Still, many students feel very pressured when test time comes around. This is an unavoidable reality of test taking, no matter what your age. There are some great ways to beat the anxiety and stress that seem to come up as you count the days leading up to a test, and they are very easy to follow. First, we'll look at some current problems for students your age and talk about how stress affects them the most. Then we'll go over how to reduce the feelings of anxiety and stress before and during a test. Finally, we'll talk about some great ways you can keep your body and mind active while you're not studying. There are so many ways to keep yourself thinking positively that you'll never worry about a test again!

FEELINGS ABOUT TAKING TESTS

WHENEVER YOUR TEACHER ANNOUNCES A test, you'll often hear a general groan from the class, and everyone will act upset. This is all part of being a student. Believe it or not, *everyone* (not only you) dreads taking tests. Many people experience feelings of anxiety or panic when it comes closer to the time of the test and may not be willing to admit their fears. You can assess whether or not you're at risk for high stress and anxiety at test time by answering a few simple questions:

✓   *When you know you have a test coming, do you put off studying in favor of other activities?*

✓   *Are you often sweating or having feelings of panic when you start a test?*

✓   *Have you thoroughly studied the material you're going to be tested on?*

✓   *Do you often tell yourself, "I don't have to worry about this now" or "I'll do just fine without studying"?*

✓   *When you last took a test, did you feel strong emotions like wanting to cry, feeling angry or frustrated or even a little bit sick to your stomach, or experiencing severe headaches?*

If you answered yes to *any* of the questions above, you're probably experiencing some anxiety issues when it comes to tests. That's okay. It can be managed by carefully looking at your triggers and how you can prepare yourself effectively. More often than not, the feelings of stress and anxiety that come with taking a test have one main root cause: You simply are not prepared! If you can go into a test and feel confident about all the preparation you've done leading up to it, taking the test will be a piece of cake. If

you're concerned about something you may not have learned or studied, it can take away your feelings of confidence. But if you've studied, there are a few things you can do right before a test that will help you get through it.

✓ **Bring a bottle of water** with you so you stay hydrated and focused during the test. If you're nervous and sweating, you may lose a lot of water your body needs in order to focus.

✓ **Arrive five or ten minutes *before* the test** to go over important study notes and the summary sheets you created. If you have a class before your test, ask the teacher to briefly go over some core concepts for everyone before the test begins.

✓ **Do the easiest problems first.** When you get the test, make sure to write your name and then read through every single problem. Don't worry about time at this point. You first need to identify the easiest questions and answer them first. The harder questions will probably be worth more points, so it's important that you have enough time at the end of the test to get them done.

✓ **Pace yourself and don't rush.** Don't constantly look at the clock or fidget with your pencil while staring blankly at the page. You have a time limit, but don't rush yourself. If you end up rushing, you may have feelings of panic. By pacing yourself, you can focus on the hardest questions near the end.

✓ **Always read the questions carefully and answer them as best you can.** When a teacher designs questions and tells you how many points each one is worth, that means he or she is looking for very specific answers. If a question is worth five points and asks you to explain a lot, your teacher is probably looking for five very specific parts in your answer. This can help you narrow down the choices when you're writing out your answer.

✓ **Keep your eyes on your own paper and refrain from cheating.** Cheating or glancing over at someone's paper may seem like a good idea, especially if you're feeling as though you might fail the test, but you must never cheat! Even if you fail a test, your teacher may give you the opportunity to do it over. But if you cheat, you'll probably lose the opportunity to retake the test.

✓ **Prepare a breakfast the night *before*.** Get a parent or sibling to help you put together a well-rounded meal. This will help you prepare your body *and* mind beforehand. It's very important to have a lot of energy when you take a test. This can be applied to every part of the day as well. A well-rounded meal may help decrease any nervous feelings you have beforehand.

✓ **Take some deep breaths before and during your test.** And remember, it's just a test. No matter how you end up doing, it won't be the end of the world if you don't do well. You can always talk to your teacher after you're done if you feel you didn't do well. Your teacher will often provide you with the opportunity to go over your answers and make the necessary corrections. Even if you're not given the chance to make corrections, having the correct answers can help you on future tests.

THOUGHTS ON TEST PREP AND ANXIETY

IN THE END, THERE'S SO much you can do to prepare yourself for a test. With the tips outlined in this chapter, you should be able to make a plan that covers all kinds of different studying routines.

Remembering to plan the time beforehand and make a note of the test date as soon as you learn about it is a super-important piece of information for the future. These two things can greatly reduce test anxiety.

Although you may need some practice with developing a great study routine, once you have your own plan down, it will become easy to develop something you can use for every test that comes your way.

Remember to use your connections! Always talk to teachers if you're having trouble with questions, content, or assignments because you never know when a test will be announced. Talk to parents and classmates about having study sessions or times when you can go over the content with someone else who can help you learn. By forming a study group in your class, you can eliminate a lot of the stress that comes with studying all by yourself.

Using the tips that work for you will help reduce or even eliminate your test-taking anxiety. However, don't be alarmed if your symptoms of pre-test stress continue. It's very difficult to eliminate all those feelings with just one test. Practice these tips every time you take a quiz or test, and eventually you will stop feeling stressed out. And then you'll really find success!

Remember to focus on what you *do* know and use that to your advantage. Just because you may not be doing well in a subject doesn't mean you aren't good at it. And don't beat yourself up about it, either! Many tweens have trouble forming good study and anti-anxiety habits, so remember that like all good things, putting these ideas into practice takes time and effort. By making it fun and exciting, test taking will become a way for you to show just how much you know, and that's not scary at all!

CONCLUSION

You did it! You've arrived! You actually just finished reading this entire book. Way to go! It's a real accomplishment, when you think about it. You just read a pretty significant book that's all about what you can do to be more successful in school. That tells me something really important about you. It tells me you really do want to do better in life, whether in school or at home. And figuring out how to manage your time more efficiently so you're able to do everything you need and want to do is the first step.

By reading this book, you just learned a huge number of tips and strategies for ramping up your academic success. Don't worry if you can't remember all of them right now—I don't expect you to have a photographic memory, after all. But you still have the book to look back through whenever you need to find a particular strategy or tip to help with whatever you're struggling with.

Just keep this book handy throughout the school year. If you follow many of the tips I've shared, you will definitely become a much more successful student and a person everyone recognizes as being interested in making improvements.

When you start making awesome grades on your assignments and tests, some of the other kids in your classes might be curious and ask you how you're doing it. Now, it might be tempting to make up a story like ... you were abducted by aliens and they gave you super-schoolwork powers ... but really you can just tell them about this book, and they can get it for themselves and give the tips a try. Whatever you do, DON'T give this book away! If you let someone borrow it, make sure to set a date when he or she will return it to you. After all, you're going to want to keep using it! And remember to mark your calendar because you're going to read it again before school starts the next time around.

Good luck in all that you do—you're on your way to a bright future!

AUTHOR ERAINNA WINNETT

ERAINNA WAS BORN AND RAISED in central Louisiana. The oldest of five children she always yearned to be a teacher and forced her siblings to play school year round. Naturally, she graduated with a teaching degree in 1995 and earned her master's degree in 2000. Five years later she earned her education specialist degree in early childhood education. After fifteen years in the classroom, she moved to the role of school counselor and has never been happier.

While serving as school counselor at an elementary school in northeast Texas, she frequently uses children's books as therapy to help her students heal, learn and grow. Ideas for her books come from the students she works with on a daily basis. Her goal, as an author, is to touch the hearts of children, one story at a time. Erainna lives on a 300 acre cattle ranch near the Red River with her husband, two daughters, three dogs, two horses, and one ill-tempered cat.

To see more books by Erainna, please visit her counseling website counselingwithheart.com.

TWEEN SUCCESS SERIES ALSO INCLUDES:

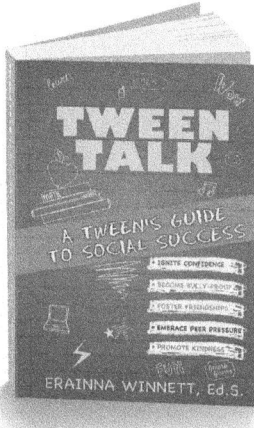

TWEEN TALK:
A TWEEN'S GUIDE to SOCIAL SUCCESS

Child education and counseling expert Erainna Winnett brings more than 20 years of experience in teaching, counseling, and raising children to the hot-button issues every tween faces today.

Written in a conversational style and chock full of concrete steps and tips, this interactive guide helps children make a smoother transition from pre-teen to teen by equipping them with proven strategies for social success.

Although *Tween Talk* was written with a tween reading audience in mind, parents, guardians, teachers, and other adults will find it an invaluable tool for supporting the children in their lives to navigate the trials and tribulations of being a tween with flying colors!

Tween Talk has chapters devoted to the following issues: Self-Confidence, Friendship, Cliques, Conflict Resolution, Peer Pressure, Bullying, Cyberbullying, and Self- Empowerment.

Also from Erainna Winnett... **Girl Power** series

Cyber Friend? Olivia and Grace are best friends, but when Olivia accidentally hurts her friend's feelings, Grace takes out her frustrations online. Olivia is shocked by the cyberbullying and even more hurt when the entire school laughs at her over something Grace posted. Can the two girls work it out? Will they ever learn to be cyber friends? This full-color story includes activities to help tween girls learn about cyberbullying, understand appropriate Internet communication, and deal with the effects of cyberbullying. ISBN 0615907725

Frenemy Jungle Ashley likes hanging out with her small group of friends at school, but they aren't always nice—especially Marcy, who often says hurtful things. Ashley is confused about Marcy's indirect put-downs until she meets an unusual and wise teacher. Can this teacher help Ashley learn the difference between a frenemy and a true friend? This full-color story offers a unique approach to one of the most pressing problems of our time ... relational aggression among tween girls. Included are easy-to-understand activities that foster self-reflection about relational aggression and teach girls how to create healthy, affirming friendships. ISBN 0615907717

Friendship Tug-of-War Stephanie loves her two best friends, Emma and Claire, and she's excited when Emma invites her to an upcoming sleepover. But when Stephanie learns that Emma didn't invite Claire, she finds herself in the middle of their fight. She has to choose one or the other—or risk losing them both. How will she get her friends to stop putting her in the middle of a friendship tug-of-war? And will they ever learn to get along? This full-color story includes activities to help girls learn about healthy boundaries in friendships and strategies for handling disagreements. ISBN 0615911773

It's Good to Be Me Brittany sees lots of great things about her best friend, but she doesn't see anything good about herself. She strikes out during softball, she's the last girl invited to a classmate's birthday party, and she isn't sure anyone really likes her. Mom sees that Brittany is having a hard time and helps her do something about it. Together they make a special box—one that will show Brittany all the great things about herself. It doesn't take long for Brittany to realize that it really is good to be her! This full-color story includes engaging activities and thought-provoking questions designed to foster self-awareness and self-confidence. ISBN 0615907709

To view book trailers, please visit http://counselingwithheart.com

www.ingramcontent.com/pod-product-compliance
Lightning Source LLC
Chambersburg PA
CBHW072354090426
42741CB00012B/3035